DIVORCE INSIGHTS

*Conversations With America's Leading
Divorce Professionals*

DIVORCE INSIGHTS
Conversations With America's Leading Divorce Professionals

Featuring:

PHILIP ALAN GREENBERG, ESQ.

DMITRIY BORSHCHAK

SUSAN GUTHRIE, ESQ.

BETH WIBERG BARBOSA, ESQ.

JOSEPH F. EMMERTH IV, ESQ.

SHANNON HOLLAND, CFP(R), CDFA™, AIF(R)

Remarkable Press™

The publisher is donating all royalties from the retail sales of **"DIVORCE INSIGHTS: CONVERSATIONS WITH AMERICA'S LEADING DIVORCE PROFESSIONALS"** to Global Autism Project:

AUTISM KNOWS NO BORDERS;
FORTUNATELY NEITHER DO WE.®

Global autism project 501(C)3, is a nonprofit organization which provides training to local individuals in evidence-based practice for individuals with autism.

Global autism project believes that every child has the ability to learn and their potential should not be limited by geographical bounds.

The global autism project seeks to eliminate the disparity in service provision seen around the world by providing high-quality training to individuals providing services in their local community. This training is made sustainable through regular training trips and contiguous remote training.

You can learn more about Global Autism Project by visiting GlobalAutismProject.org

Divorce Insights / Mark Imperial —1st ed.

Managing Editor/ Shannon Buritz

ISBN-13: 978-1-7323763-2-8

CONTENTS

A NOTE TO THE READER

Thank you for buying your copy of "DIVORCE INSIGHTS: Conversations With America's Leading Divorce Professionals." This book was originally created as a series of live interviews, that's why it reads like a series of conversations, rather than a traditional book that talks at you.

I wanted you to feel as though the participants and I are talking with you, much like a close friend, or relative, and felt that creating the material this way would make it easier for you to grasp the topics and put them to use quickly, rather than wading through hundreds of pages.

So relax, grab a pen and paper, take notes and get ready to learn some fascinating, Divorce Insights.

Warmest regards,

Mark Imperial
Publisher, Author and Radio Personality

INTRODUCTION

"DIVORCE INSIGHTS: Conversations With America's Leading Divorce Professionals" is a collaborative book series featuring leading Divorce Professionals from across the country.

Remarkable Press™ would like to extend a heartfelt thank you to all participants who took the time to submit their chapter and offer their support in becoming ambassadors for this project.

100% of the royalties from the retail sales of this book will be donated to Global Autism Project. Should you want to make a direct donation, visit their website at: GlobalAutismProject.org

PHILIP GREENBERG

Life After Divorce

Conversation with Philip Greenberg

Tell us a little bit about yourself and the type of clients that you serve:

Philip Greenberg: My journey begins at Brooklyn College back in 1969 when it was still tuition free. I was passionate about politics and was elected student body president. You could say I was the Bernie Sanders of Brooklyn College because I ran as an independent against entrenched student parties on a populous platform...and I won. It was a memorable moment in my life because even the local congressman's chief aid called me at home to congratulate me. After heading up numerous organizations at Brooklyn College, I entered NYU law school. I passed the New York bar exam on my very first try in 1974 and continued in the same fashion to pass the New Jersey bar in 1988. I have been practicing in New York and New Jersey ever since with small law firms. In late 2000, I decided to fly solo and set up my own practice.

The clients that I currently help are divorcing couples. Growing up, I always loved to watch Divorce Court on television. I grew up in a neighborhood where everyone had two parents because we were all too poor to get divorced and too poor to die. So, I was fascinated by the topic of divorce and started out representing husbands and fathers specifically. I was very aware of the fact that the men on Divorce Court always seemed to get the raw end of the deal. Being passionate about civil rights, I wanted to represent these men and protect their rights. I also began representing women very successfully in the late 1970s when I received a call from a good friend who wanted me to represent his sister-in-law in a divorce. I referred them elsewhere as I was not representing women at the time, but they didn't particularly like the referrals and begged me to reconsider. I did and have been representing both men and women ever since. The only client I will turn down is one who is planning to use the children as weapons in the divorce. I don't draw very many lines, but this is a circumstance that I absolutely will not tolerate.

With that being said, I pride myself on many years of experience. I am very knowledgeable and patient, which is invaluable when dealing with divorcing couples. It is important to remember that divorcing clients are going through one of the most difficult times of their lives. They need a lawyer who is understanding and available. I am one of those attorneys who never goes on vacation. I am always available to meet the needs of my clients.

What is the number one most common concern that clients have when they first consult with you?

Philip Greenberg: One of the most common concerns involves the well-being of the children. I have many clients who fear that the other parent will not be a suitable custodial parent and the main concern becomes getting custody. In situations where both are fit parents, my clients are overwhelmed at how to still be involved in the lives of the children without having their partner in the picture any longer. Especially when talking about children who are under the age of 18, clients are worried about maintaining the same relationship with the kids after the dust has settled and the divorce is final.

For couples who don't have children or whose children are grown up, their main concern tends to be financial security. For example, I was in Queens Supreme court last week dealing with a 55-year marriage. My client is 79 and his wife is 80. Obviously, their children are all grown up, so their worries are strictly financial. In any case, it is my job to advocate for these clients and quell their concerns to make the divorce process as smooth as possible.

What do you feel is one of the biggest myths out there when it comes to the divorce process?

Philip Greenberg: Throughout my career, I have been hearing the same thing for decades..." Well, you know, marriage is just a piece of paper and if it doesn't work out, you just get divorced." The attitude seems very nonchalant and many young people these days think that divorce is not such a big deal. The truth of the matter is, divorce has repercussions. The impact it has on parents and children can very well govern that relationship for the rest of their lives. Not to mention, there are financial implications. I have seen men who will spend the rest of their lifetime in the negative when it comes to finances due to alimony and child support payments. These men often are only able to remarry women who have money because they can't even afford to maintain a new relationship. These are extremely hard truths that divorcing couples are faced with.

What are some of the most common fears people have about beginning the divorce process and how can they get past these fears?

Philip Greenberg: Especially when it comes to the fathers, they are concerned about being removed from the lives of their children. They fear being reduced to simply "a check in the mail" and may have

heard horror stories from friends going through similar situations. Fathers also fear whether they will be able to maintain financial stability. Will the burdens of the divorce carry forward for the rest of their lives? For example, will they be able to afford to remarry, have more children, or even afford retirement? A common statement I hear during consultations is "I am here to figure out whether or not I can afford to get divorced."

In order to get past these fears, first and foremost, they need to be very selective about the lawyer they choose to hire. Especially in cases where the decision is being made for them and the other spouse is filing for divorce, the most important decision to make is who the lawyer will be and whether they are qualified to handle the particular situation. For example, a man wants full custody of his children, hires and pays big money to a lawyer, only to find out that the lawyer believes that "a child's place is really with the mother." You must find a lawyer from the start who has beliefs that align with your goals and will work to help you achieve them. In order to quell fears before they even begin, get your ducks in a row as soon as the word "divorce" is mentioned. Set up a consultation and let a professional guide you through what to expect and set you on a path for a smooth transition into the next phase of your life.

What is a little-known pitfall or common mistake that you see couples make on the road to divorce?

Philip Greenberg: The biggest mistake that I find men making is before the lawyers are even hired, they'll make certain commitments to their wives, such as..."no matter how this turns out you're going to get the house." When men are making these promises, they are often unaware of other things that may come into play once sitting down with a lawyer. Then it turns into "When I promised you the house, I didn't realize I would also have to share my pension with you." It is a bad idea to make any sort of agreements before sitting down with a knowledgeable attorney. I have seen this happen in cases where children are involved as well. Dad promises that they will get to live in the same house and go to the same schools. It all plays out and dad realizes he is unable to keep these promises based on the financial situation it will put him in. In the end, it saves the entire family a lot of hurt and stress to make agreements and commitments alongside an attorney who can guide the process and help manage expectations.

Can you share a lesson that you learned early on that still impacts how you do business today?

Philip Greenberg: There is no denying the fact that I am an eternal optimist. So, when I first started out, I would tend to "over-promise" to my clients. I was also idealistic and naive, which to some extent, I still am. I would go to the bank with whatever information my client gave me, fully believing they were not suppressing facts or withholding information that would be bad for their case. As it turns out, many clients won't reveal certain truths because they fear you will not take them on. So, I would often over-promise in terms of results, or how long it would take, or the cost because I did not have all the facts.

I find that many lawyers are better at being salesmen than looking out for the best interest of their client. They promise things in order to keep the clients with deep pockets, knowing they will not be able to deliver on those promises. For example, they might promise a man who has been married for 25 years to a non-working wife that he will not have to pay alimony. And after he has paid the lawyer a hefty fee based on this promise, the lawyer says "Well, I did not realize that she is unemployable" or "I didn't realize she was unemployed for the ENTIRE 25 years you were married", at which point alimony is unavoidable.

Today, I pride myself on not over-promising to my clients. When I teach other lawyers, I always stress the importance of this. It will only result in an unhappy client. I make it a point to start out conversations with... "based on what you told me". This helps manage expectations and holds the client responsible for providing accurate information. In my practice, I work diligently to give my clients an accurate picture of what to expect and value open lines of communication and honesty.

What is the most important thing divorcing couples should consider when evaluating a family law attorney?

Philip Greenberg: By far, the most important thing is that the lawyer should be in sync with your goals. You should feel very comfortable with the attorney that you hire. When dealing with issues such as kids and money, especially in New York, the case could last a matter of years. So, you never want to hire someone who you dread picking up the phone and calling. Similarly to doctors, a lawyer should have excellent "bedside manner". They should be able to make even the most stressful, critical situation better by having the ability to reassure and understand their clients. Finally, make sure you have a lawyer that is experienced, knowledgeable, and dealt with enough complex cases that they are able to deliver results.

How can someone find out more about you and how you can help?

Philip Greenberg: I have a website www.philipgreenberg.com that can give potential clients a good feel for what I am all about. This is a really great place to start. I have also had several clients track me down on Super Lawyers, which offers the top 5% of family lawyers in New York. I look forward to helping you realize that there truly can be life after divorce.

PHILIP ALAN GREENBERG, ESQ.

Divorce and Family Law Attorney and

Civil Litigator

Philip Greenberg was born in Brooklyn, New York and is a genuine post-World War II baby boomer, not just because he was born between 1946 and 1968, but his parents met in North Africa during the war (his father was an American soldier and his mother was a local Tunisian; he sent for her after the war).

He is a "product" of the New York City public school system, including Erasmus High School (he had the same music teacher as Barbara Streisand; his name was Mr. Bowden, and claimed to be the one who taught her how to sing). After that, Philip attended Brooklyn College, when it was still tuition-free. His "crowning achievement" at Brooklyn College was running for student body president his senior year. Philip ran as an independent against entrenched student parties and was elected and served as president in his senior year. Philip then went on to N.Y.U. Law School, carrying out the decision he made at age 12 to

become a lawyer. While in law school, he joined Phi Alpha Delta Law Fraternity International, the leading professional law fraternity in the world. He continues to be active in Phi Alpha Delta, some 48 years after being initiated. Among other things, Philip was elected and served on the International Tribunal (their equivalent of the Supreme Court) of the law fraternity, as well as having been elected and served as a member of the International Executive Board.

Philip is also active in organizations such as the Freemasons, he is a member of Maimonides-Marshall Lodge #739; among other positions, he was Master of his lodge four times, as well as the President of the Sixth Manhattan District.

He is currently a Trustee of what is now known as the Chelsea Shul, which is one of the oldest continuous Jewish congregations in the United States. Politically, Philip is a registered Democrat. When he lived in Brooklyn and later in Manhattan, Philip was elected to lower level party positions within the local Democratic parties in Kings (Brooklyn), and New York County.

Philip has been a member of the New York Bar since 1974 and the New Jersey Bar since 1988. He is also a member of the Federal Bars, including the Federal District Courts in New York and New Jersey, the Second Circuit Court of Appeals, and the U.S. Supreme Court. In his early years as an attorney, his emphasis was on international law and civil litigation. While he has continued to handle civil litigation for at least the last quarter of a century, his emphasis has been on family law, primarily New York and New Jersey divorces, as well as Family Court cases throughout New York. Over the years, Philip has won some notable Appellate Decisions and trial level cases in the divorce field, and in other areas of law. For example, in 1975 he won an Appellate case called 943 Lexington vs. Niarchos (having to do with regulations of cooperative apartments), in 1988 Cross vs. Cross (still a leading case on common law marriage), and in 2009 Fullman vs. R & G Brenner (having to do with restrictive covenants). After spending decades in small law firms, on November 1, 2000, Philip opened his current solo practice. He is associated with some former law partners and has counsels who work on some cases collaboratively.

Among his professional honors, Philip was chosen for Super Lawyers (top 5% of New York divorce lawyers), A-V rated (highest rating for ability and ethics) since the mid-1980's by Martindale Hubbell, and is in "Who's Who in American Law" and "Who's Who in America" (winning the Lifetime Achievement Award).

As for his personal life, Philip followed his own advice and "married his second wife first". The result of marrying for the first (and only) time in his late forties is that he is still happily married to   his "trophy wife", Cheryl Greenberg.

WEBSITE: www.philipagreenberg.com

EMAIL: Lawman802@aol.com

ADDRESS: 10 Park Avenue, Suite 2A, New York, N. Y.

10016

OFFICE: 212-279-4550

FAX: 212-279-0466

DMITRIY BORSHCHAK

The Power of Advocacy in Family Matters

Conversation with Dmitriy Borshchak

Tell us about how you are helping your clients:

Dmitriy Borshchak: My firm is a full-service civil litigation firm, specifically focusing on family law matters. These include, but are not limited to; divorce, legal separation, child custody, and child support. We help people with issues concerning family. As well as divorcing couples, we see couples who may not be married but share a child together. An issue that may arise in this situation is one parent wanting to move to another state due to an employment opportunity. The other parent lives here. Obviously, this is a huge impact on the child. We would focus on the child and how we can help minimize the effects of relocation if, and when it occurs.

In a divorce context, we often see two people who had a lengthy marriage and were really, really happy at one point. But now they've come to a stage in their lives where they're just finding themselves to be incompatible and they need to separate. At this point, emotions are flaring. There are so many emotions. The entire field is emotionally driven. We strive to provide sound advice and minimize the risks that our client is exposed to, both in the present time and five to ten years down the road. Though we primarily focus on family law matters, occasionally these matters lead to other issues such as wills and estates that we can help our clients with as well.

What is the most common concern or challenge that you hear from clients when they first come to see you?

Dmitriy Borshchak: In this field, a client is typically coming to me with multiple concerns. When it comes to family law matters, the stakes could not be higher. It isn't as simple as a breach of contract, for example, where somebody promised to build a fence, they failed to build the fence, and now they owe the money back to the person that paid them for their services. Family law matters are not about money. There is no big judgement. There is no jury.

At the end of the day, these cases involve two parents who are entrenched in their position as the better parent to have custody. The person who has custody makes the most important decisions regarding their child such as where they go to school, when they eat, when they sleep, what religion they practice, etc. Often a client's main concern is whether they will "win" custody. I hear that question almost every single time. It is an impossible question to answer because what is the definition of "winning" in a child custody proceeding? There isn't one. There might be a view of what winning would look like...one parent is granted custody, the other is not. But that is not a "win" when it creates friction between the parties. Litigation tends to cause parents to dislike each other even more than before the process began.

A chief concern is usually "how much is this going to cost?" This question is difficult to answer, mainly because of so many factors outside of my control, let alone the client's control. During the litigation process, a parent may file frivolous documents with the court, often seeking emergency custody based on allegations that are unfounded, untrue, and eventually dismissed. Requests for emergency custody are generally conducted ex-parte, meaning the other party or parent is not there to defend themselves against the claims alleged. Nevertheless, it is the court's duty to take these allegations seriously. The court must do this as they should. The court must be proactive, and emergency custody is generally granted in hopes of preventing a possible bad situation. For example, let's say Parent A files an emergency custody motion requesting custody of the child because Parent B overdosed on opioids and left the child unattended for hours without attention. Even if these allegations are untrue, based on these alleged facts, the motion is routinely granted. Now, Parent B will have to prepare to address these allegations in court. At the full hearing, the allegations are found to be untrue and the motion is dismissed. The next thing you know, Parent B receives a bill that they did not expect. In Parent B's mind, they did not do anything wrong; the allegations were false, why are they responsible for these fees? Unforeseen allegations are exactly as they sound... unforeseen. Without knowing what the other side is willing and not willing to do or say, it is extremely difficult to quote a definite sum for costs of taking the case and necessary litigation.

In custody cases, clients struggle with the notion of "how are we going to do this for the next 16 to 18 years," when the other parent is impossible to communicate with. When people come to me for help, it is generally because of a dispute, or in other words a disagreement with the other party. It is hard for people to fathom the stress of dealing with these issues until the child is an adult. In this case, my answer is always..." I will be by your side. My entire staff will be by your side." This is why we focus on long term risks, so that anything you could possibly be faced with in the future is addressed right away. For example, in the case of a child who is four years old at the time, we address provisions that involve high school years (costs, extra-curricular activities, driver's license, alcohol, drugs, etc.). We pride ourselves in ensuring that long-term concerns, even those many years from now, are addressed now, and not when they come up years down the line.

What do you feel are the biggest myths or misconceptions out there when it comes to divorce?

Dmitriy Borshchak: One of the biggest misconceptions that I hear comes from men that have a child outside of marriage. Whether they heard it from a friend or saw it on Google, they believe that because they are paying child support, they are automatically entitled to custodial rights and decision-making authority regarding the child. The truth of the matter is, in Ohio, the father does not have any rights until he petitions the court to allocate his parental rights and responsibilities.

Another misconception exists that applies to both males and females. One partner will often believe that everything in the other partner's name is solely theirs and they are not entitled to any of it. In Ohio, everything acquired during the marriage is marital property unless it is separate property. Especially when it comes to marriages of long duration, there is a great deal of marital property to be taken into consideration.

Another myth that I often hear involves spousal support or alimony, as most people coin it. Some believe that because one spouse agreed to stay home and raise the children, they are not entitled to support because it was a voluntary decision. They agreed to the arrangement, so they are out of luck. It is not the most common myth, but certainly one of the most preposterous ones.

A knowledgeable family law attorney can help dispel these misconceptions once and for all and ensure that all parties walk away with what they are entitled to. This makes for a less stressful transition into life after divorce.

What are the most common fears that clients come to you with?

Dmitriy Borshchak: One of the biggest fears when it comes to divorce is "how am I going to survive?" Many people don't conceptualize it through, but when you divorce, you are splitting the marital unit in half. Thus, income becomes the source for much of the anxiety. This rings particularly true when I am representing the spouse that stayed at home.

I address this fear by narrowly focusing on negotiation while keeping the client's chief objective in mind. My financial and tax background allows me to look down the road five to ten years and focus on what we can do to ensure future financial security and stability five or so years after litigation has concluded. For example, there is a marital estate that includes a house with no mortgage. It is worth about $250,000, if sold. In addition, there is a pension that is worth $300,000 but does not vest until retirement. This means that neither party can touch the money until a date certain in the future. The fifty-thousand-dollar difference becomes irrelevant when thinking about the liquidity of the asset, and even more so the timing of its access. With a house, you may qualify for a home-equity line of credit allowing you to borrow against your own asset. With most pensions, you cannot do that. A parent who has been a stay-at-home parent their entire life may not want to pursue the pension because of the lack of access to immediate funds, while the other would want to retain their pension because of compounding interest. Not all situations are similar, but the point is that you must consider all scenarios and all factors while keeping the client's exposure to risk in mind, both in the now, and in the future.

We work very hard and diligently during negotiations to quell the fears associated with income. I pride myself on the level of preparation I undertake not only prior to starting negotiations, but before I accept a case. I strive to know the case like the back of my hand, so I can anticipate exactly what the client needs before they even tell me.

Another common fear that some clients have is "what will happen to my business during the divorce?" For example, some couples want to split the family owned business 50/50. They do not wish to liquidate the business and they want to continue a working relationship. Though that sounds difficult, it does happen. So, we take time drafting agreements, and stipulations addressing hypothetical issues that may arise during the joint business venture.

I take both fears and concerns extremely seriously. The more prepared I can be, the more at ease my clients will feel as they see the options presented to them. I will not only provide courses of action, but also the possible consequences of these actions and decisions. By giving my clients the "big picture", I am able to guide them through the very real fears that occur during the divorce process.

What are some of the little-known pitfalls or common mistakes that you see couples make on the road to divorce?

Dmitriy Borshchak: The most common mistake people make is talking about the case with their children. That is the worst thing parents can do. Generally speaking, adults don't even understand the divorce process. They certainly cannot expect the children to comprehend it. Parents often don't consider the negative effects of telling their children about the litigation process. The kids become scared and confused about who they are going to live with and how their lives are going to change. The court certainly frowns upon children being put in the middle of a divorce. One of the first things I say to a new client is that their children are not to be included in any discussions regarding the case.

It goes without saying that the family law arena is emotionally driven, and it takes a lot of preparation to keep these emotions in check. This not only involves preparing myself, but preparing my clients for hearings, trials, etc. I do my best to ensure that my clients are informed of what they can expect in court. I take them through everything from cross examinations to courtroom rules, to communicating with their spouse outside of court. When communication and negotiation take place between parties outside of court, one party often unknowingly negotiates all our leverage away. Therefore, it is so important for clients to allow their attorneys to represent them, and act as their voice box.

What inspired you to get into family law?

Dmitriy Borshchak: I immigrated to the United States when I was about four years young after my parents got a divorce in the Ukraine. My mother had a great attorney helping her through the process, which ignited my interest in the legal field, particularly in an advocate role. I vividly remember when my parents were separating, as divorce is very difficult in the Ukraine. At the time, you had to get permission from the other spouse to leave the country. My mother and I were making a huge move and we couldn't have done it without her attorney. I recall sleeping at her home because she was safeguarding our passport. She never left my mother's side until the day we got on the plane and flew to Cleveland, Ohio. This is where my initial inspiration began.

I worked in a clinic while in law school, helping Ohio residents with very low income. They were going through extremely difficult custody and divorce issues. One mother lost custody because the paternal grandmother alleged abuse and violence in front of the child which was completely unfounded. I realized what an impact I could have when I was successful in reuniting the child with the mother, witnessing her cry tears of joy for a half hour without interruption; I will never forget this moment. It is moments like these that remind me that I have found the role that I am destined to be in.

I love what I do. I genuinely love what I do. I look forward to it every single day, even on the weekends. I enjoy working on the weekends because I am able to work in peace. It sounds strange but during the regular week it is difficult because emergencies come up routinely, and at those times you have no other choice than to drop what you are doing and address the problem. I love that I can make a direct impact. The inspiration came from my roots when I was coming to the United States. And it grew over the years. I am truly inspired by working with people, addressing their problems, and solving the problems. At the end of the day, that's what lawyers are. We are paid problem solvers. We solve problems with the clients' best interests in mind and always ensure their risk is diminished both short term and long term.

Is there any other important advice you can offer couples on the path to divorce?

Dmitriy Borshchak: If you have children, whether you're going through a divorce or a custody case, don't lose sight of how the case is affecting them. Most couples come into a divorce or litigation only thinking about themselves, and their highly charged emotions. It is important to consider the short-term and long-term side effects when you are doing things such as talking poorly about your soon to be ex-partner in front of the children.

Another piece of important advice involves the appropriate way to respond to your spouse's negativity. Remember when the other party says something to upset you, and they get a reaction or response, you are giving them exactly what they were hoping for. A reaction. I have seen several cases of spousal abuse that started simply by the controlling spouse seeking, and always getting a reaction. For example, abusers and narcissists get control over someone over a period of time by convincing them that they are not worth anything. They make demands and thrive off the reaction to meet whatever those demands are. I have one client that I have been coaching for the last four months and she has been living with the father of her child for twelve years. He had absolute control over her. She would walk on eggshells everyday...even closing the dishwasher too loudly would upset him. I received an email from her the other day thanking me because she "had never felt so free." This is one of the many reasons I find it so important to coach my clients on reactions and responses.

How can people find out more about your practice and get in contact with you?

Dmitriy Borshchak: They can visit my website at www.dlbcounsel.com. I can be reached via phone at (614) 334-6851. The practice address is 1650 Lake Shore Drive, Suite 150, Columbus, OH 43204. I encourage prospective clients to read my reviews in order to get an idea of what is like to work with me on a case from start to finish. I look forward to being your advocate.

DMITRIY BORSHCHAK

Family Lawyer

*Founding Attorney of the Law Office of
Dmitriy Borshchak*

Dmitriy Borshchak is a dedicated family lawyer in Columbus and founding attorney of The Law Office of Dmitriy Borshchak. After first pursuing a brief career in medicine, Dmitriy found his true passion in the legal field, assisting clients and helping them navigate tough situations. At the firm, Dmitriy assists clients with a broad range of complex legal matters, including divorce, child custody, child support, marital agreements, fathers' rights, spousal support, and more. With every case he takes on, Dmitriy works to manage and minimize his clients' financial and legal risk. He employs a personalized, methodical approach in order to provide clients with the clear, straightforward answers and advice they need. No matter how difficult a case may be, Dmitriy is committed to aggressively advocating for his clients' rights and best interests.

Dmitriy obtained his undergraduate degree in Political Science from Ohio University. There, he joined the student senate and began investigating how he could personally help the local community and students. He went on to attend law school at Capital University Law School in Columbus, Ohio. During his time there, Dmitriy was a member of the American Association for Justice Mock Trial Team, was on the Dean's List, and received the CALI Award for Business and Financial Concepts for Lawyers. During his time in law school, he also worked pro bono, representing individuals in the Capital University Law School Litigation Clinic who could not afford an attorney at no charge.

Dmitriy began his law career at the Franklin County Prosecutor's Office while still in law school. There, he focused his practice on felonies while simultaneously working as a supervised assistant prosecutor at Hilliard's Mayor's Court. He also gained invaluable experience working at the consulting firm of Milegroup Consulting in Mayfield Village, Ohio. There, Dmitriy gained concrete experience dealing with financial risk-knowledge he uses today to help his clients foresee and pinpoint issues that his clients may face.

Dmitriy's legal experience also encompasses time spent working as a Law Clerk at Kats Law in Shaker Heights, Ohio, where he primarily handled matters relating to personal injury claims, including correspondence with insurance companies, meeting with clients, and compiling demand packets.

In 2016, Dmitriy joined Weis & O'Connor, LLC in Columbus, Ohio, first as a Law Clerk and later as an Associate of the firm. During his time there, Dmitry gained extensive experience preparing and drafting pleadings on behalf of clients, responding to opposing counsels' motions, advising clients on various family law issues, and more. He learned how to help clients understand the inherent risks involved in their case, as well as how to manage those risks. Today, Dmitriy uses this insight to help clients avoid and/or diminish the risk to liability, as well as financial risks associated with their situation.

WEBSITE: www.dlbcounsel.com

EMAIL: dmitriy@dlbcounsel.com

PHONE: (614) 334-6851

ADDRESS: 1650 Lake Shore Drive, Suite 150, Columbus, OH 43204

SUSAN GUTHRIE

THE RESOLUTION REVOLUTION

Use Mindful Mediation to Resolve Your Divorce and Save Time, Money and Stress

Conversation with Susan Guthrie

Tell us about Breaking Free Mediation and how you are helping your clients.

Susan Guthrie: As a former top divorce litigator specializing in high conflict and high net worth cases, I teamed with a fellow leading divorce attorney to found

Breaking Free Mediation, Inc. in order to provide those going through the process of divorce with a less expensive, less time-consuming and less adversarial way to move through divorce. In addition, we are the first mediation service in the country to provide a mindfulness track for our clients in order to help them to manage the difficult emotions that invariably accompany the process of separation and divorce.

Divorce today is an extremely expensive, divisive and time-consuming event for most people going through the process. The average divorce in America costs approximately $27,000 PER PERSON and that average includes those that do not have attorneys because they cannot afford them. In fact, approximately 85% of cases pending in courts today have at least one party who is self-represented. While litigating, I routinely had clients who spent tens, and in some cases hundreds, of thousands of dollars on attorney's fees, experts and evaluations. Recently I even spoke with a new client who spent more than one million dollars on her divorce. Even for those who can afford counsel, that kind of price tag is hard to swallow and can affect the financial health of your family permanently. It is a truth that at a time when expenses are naturally going to increase when one household becomes two, the extraordinary expenses of traditional divorce litigation can quickly dissipate a family's savings, assets and income.

In addition, the litigation process, where both parties put their cases in the hands of attorneys to handle everything on their behalf, quickly becomes adversarial and can drag out over a very long period of time. There are a few reasons for this phenomenon but essentially, the litigation process is structured like any other lawsuit. It is Party A vs. Party B and each side "argues" for their desired outcome. There is no collaboration and little cooperation in this process. It is much more a series of motions and allegations which are divisive and polarizing as you move forward toward your final judgment. All discussion is carried out by your attorney and your input and interaction with your spouse are generally discouraged. In the end you have a judgement, but it is one that was either negotiated for you by the attorneys, or worse, imposed upon you by a judge.

I have always found it to be perplexing that people who have made all their own decisions as an adult, such as where to live, where to work and when to get married, suddenly, at the time of divorce, choose to put their lives and the lives of their children into the hands of strangers. There is no reason why most people cannot make all the decisions needed to work through the issues of their divorce together with their spouse and mediation allows you to do that. After all, who knows you and your family's needs better than you do? Who will be living according to the agreements reached in the divorce process? YOU WILL! So, doesn't it make sense that you and your spouse should make these decisions together?

That is not to say that having these conversations and making these decisions is easy to do. These are difficult conversations in most cases and generally, couples facing divorce have difficulty communicating about even relatively simple topics, let alone the major life issues around your finances and your children that you face in divorce. That is where mediation comes in. Bottom line, you should be making these major decisions about your lives and family yourself, but you need some professional help to work through the process.

Mediation is a completely different process than the traditional litigation process. First, it is entirely voluntary and you both have to choose to be there. When you both have a reason to be there together, you each have an incentive to stick with the process and to come to agreements. In mediation, you and your spouse will discuss all of the issues of your divorce directly, with the ability to have input and to express your thoughts and positions about what works best for your family in order to reach agreements that you can both live with. The mediator is there as a neutral professional to support both of you equally by giving you guidance and information about the issues that you need to address in your divorce. They also help you by facilitating those difficult conversations. Trained professional mediators have many tools for helping you to stay focused on the issues at hand rather than letting the past interrupt your progress toward resolution as you and your spouse fall into your usual patterns of disagreement. Mediators use a number of skills and methods to help the two of you work together to find the solution that feels fair to both of you.

Statistically, agreements or judgments that are reached through the litigation process, that your attorney negotiated for you or that a judge imposed on you, are not agreements that stand or that people follow. Sooner rather than later, the party who is unhappy with the orders will use any excuse to come back to court to try to modify what they don't like. I have seen this happen time and time again. This constant revisiting of the negotiation or litigation cycle keeps you in the past and prevents you from moving forward. It also continues the exhausting conflict cycle as the litigation process continues over and over again.

A major benefit of working through your divorce issues in mediation is that when you do finally arrive at an agreement it will be one that you both participated in, made decisions about what you could live with and what you could live without and what works best for your family. These agreements that you work so hard to arrive at with your spouse directly are the ones that will stick, the ones that will work and the ones that help you both move forward into the future. Even when issues do need to be revisited after the divorce is final, such as when someone loses their job or a child attains their majority, couples that mediate their divorce will also return to mediation to work out any needed changes. Just like with the original mediation, these matters are usually resolved quickly and with much less expense than going to court would entail.

Another major benefit of mediation is that through the process, you and your spouse start to establish new methods of communication which will stand you in good stead as you go forward and co-parent in the future. Most couples, by the time of divorce, have either stopped communicating or worse, only communicate by arguing and fighting. This is a cycle that is only compounded in the adversarial process and the communicating is done through the professionals so the actual people getting divorced are only learning to let others speak for them and to communicate with their ex only through others. In mediation, with the help of the mediator, people can start to break the bad habits and destructive communication patterns and begin to relate to each other in ways that are more productive and respectful. Remember, especially when you are parents, the other person will always be in your children's lives and you will need to have some interaction with them so finding a way to talk about what is important is vital for your children's wellbeing.

Finally, couples that mediate their divorce generally spend less time in the process and much less money than in a litigated divorce. This saves both your sanity and your wallet. The time of divorce is one of limbo. A time where your future, both financially and with respect to your children, is undefined and subject to negotiation. This is a very difficult state to live in for long but litigated divorces can take a year in some states to two, three, four or more in other states like California. The emotional wear and tear of living in this uncertainty while fighting for what you feel is fair is hard to describe but trust me, it is devastating. All the while, the attorneys, the experts and all the other expenses of divorce continue to mount up which can devastate even the most financially stable families. Since mediation is a streamlined process, where you and your spouse are making decisions in real time, together agreements can come together much more quickly. There is no set timeline for a mediated divorce, but the process is in your hands. If the two parties are motivated, they can schedule appointments with their mediator quickly and move through the issues at a speed that they are comfortable with. If they need a bit more time to process things or to pull together information, the process can be spread out over a longer period. The bottom line is that the participants in mediation choose the timeline for their process, not the attorneys or the courts.

Likewise, the costs are much lower in mediation because the parties are jointly paying their mediator and any other neutral professionals that might be retained. Even when the couple each have a consulting attorney during mediation, they only pay for the attorney's time when it is needed, which is usually significantly less than in a litigated matter. Overall, a mediated divorce allows more money to stay with the family which only helps everyone with the transition to two households.

What are the advantages of mediating a divorce for divorcing couples?

Susan Guthrie: Having worked with divorcing individuals and couples for such a long period, it became clear to me that the litigation process, which so many people employ when they are getting divorced, only makes a bad situation worse in many situations.

When I first started practicing law in 1990 there really was no other way to get divorced than through litigation. I joined a law firm and started working with the head of the matrimonial law division and quickly learned that every litigated divorce follows a similar pattern. First, you draft the paperwork and have a marshal serve it to the other party. Then you serve them with discovery requests for years and years of financial documents. You serve them with motions for temporary support, temporary visitation plans and other remedies to be a band aid on the situation while the divorce is pending in court. Often you would take the deposition of the other side and ask them questions under oath trying to get information or to catch them in a lie. Keep in mind, all the while the other side was likely doing the same to your client.

Once you have all the discovery done and the facts pulled together so that you know what the marital "pie" is, you then start negotiating with the other attorney to try to divide that pie up and get your client what they say they want. You send the other attorney proposals and they send counterproposals and you try to winnow it down to something palatable to each side. Throughout however, the attorneys still need to be preparing for trial because if negotiations fail, that is the only way to bring the case to a close. For those cases that do not settle before their trial date, the gloves come off and the mudslinging starts. At trial the main goal is to present the facts in a manner that will best achieve the outcome desired by the client. That usually involves tearing down the other side and revealing all those things about your spouse that you know will hurt them or show them in a bad light, but remember, they will do the same to you.

In the end, the man or woman in the black robe will listen to all that and will tell you what they think is fair under the law in your state. This is usually not what either of you were hoping for but that is what you get when you put your life in the hands of a stranger.

If that process doesn't sound destructive and adversarial to you, go back and read it again because this is one of the most exhausting and soul-crushing things that I have seen people go through and I was a participant in this process for many years of my career.

I had been frustrated for years with the divorce litigation process, as I saw client after client, and family after family destroyed financially and emotionally after the rigors and trauma of the divorce. Trust me, you do not pick up the phone to talk to your ex about one of the kids having trouble in class when you have torn each other apart during the divorce. In the end, everyone loses and unfortunately the conflict cycle just continues because that is the norm that has been created.

I honestly was looking to leave the profession and find some other way to make a living and then a colleague introduced me to the idea of non-adversarial divorce and mediation. The ability to help people to separate and work through their divorce in a respectful and cooperative manner has changed my practice and my clients' lives.

What do you feel are the biggest myths out there when it comes to mediating a divorce?

Susan Guthrie: There are several myths or misconceptions about mediation that I would like to dispel. The top four are:

Myth #1: Mediation is the kinder, gentler way to divorce. I find this misconception to be very prevalent and have even heard some litigation colleagues use the phrase. It is as if they think that we are sitting around in a circle holding hands singing kumbaya. In fact, the mediation process can be difficult. You are sitting with the person that you are divorcing and talking about dividing up all your money, your debt and your children's time. In addition, things have usually happened along the way to divorce that raise high emotions. There might have been financial deception or infidelity or maybe just gradual growing apart, but that still feels like rejection in many ways. All of this makes for some difficult conversations but as I said before, the mediator is there to help you work through those difficulties and to help you to move out of the past and into the future. As I said above, there is great value in creating these new patterns of communication, especially if you will be going forward and parenting your children together. Mediation is not therapy but there often is a therapeutic effect in the process and that benefits everyone.

Myth #2: High conflict couples cannot work through their divorce in mediation. Much like Myth #1, there is a prevalent misconception that only the most amicable of couples can mediate which is just not true in my experience. In fact, while litigating, I specialized in high net worth and high conflict cases and I can say that for most high conflict cases, mediation is actually a better method for resolving the divorce than the court system is. The reason for this is twofold. First, most courts and judges are not prepared for nor do they have any specialized training or understanding of high conflict individuals or those with personality disorders such as narcissists or people with borderline personality disorder. They do not teach that stuff in law school. I have learned how to educate clients on the high conflict paradigm, and I have also worked with many, many high conflict couples to help them to resolve their differences or at least come to a detente so that they can move on. Next, the litigation process often becomes a tool in the hands of the high conflict person, and they will use the process to harass and wear down the other party. High conflict individuals will file motion after motion with little regard for the rules of court or the facts and in this manner the legal process is a hindrance and not a help to the parties. A high conflict case will usually drag out for an extraordinary length of time until either the money or the strength of one of the parties gives out and they just give in to any settlement in order to get it over with. These cases usually fare much better with an experienced mediator who can help to manage the high conflict party and to help the discussion remain focused on the essential issues of the divorce rather than all of the crazy-making allegations of the high conflict situation.

In addition, in mediation, there are methods where the parties can be separated so that they interact with their mediator but are not in the same room. This is called caucusing and the mediator usually shuttles back and forth between two rooms. Even better is online mediation which we offer at Breaking Free Mediation. The entire mediation is conducted via videoconferencing so the high conflict couple can be in completely separate locations but can still see each other and communicate directly without needing to physically be in separate rooms. It is said that 85% of communication is visual, and with online mediation that nuance is not lost while safety and security are maintained. So, converse to the misconception, in many cases, mediation is the best method for resolving a high conflict divorce.

Myth #3: The mediator is going to listen to us and then tell us what to do. Many couples come to mediation thinking that it is essentially a private courtroom and the mediator will act as the judge. This could not be further from the truth. Mediation is the opposite of the coercive litigation process and the mediator is a neutral support system for both parties, not a quasi-judge. One of the truly great advantages of the mediation process is that every decision made in mediation is made by agreement of both parties. This starts from the very first decision in any mediation which is to choose mediation as the method for resolving the divorce. I always tell clients that there is no agreement until they both agree. At a time in your life when everything feels like a loss and the future is unknown, self-advocating and working to identify what is important to you in your new future is incredibly empowering and results in the best kind of settlement: one where you both end up with as much of what is important to each of you as possible.

Myth #4: I won't get a "fair" settlement. This is by far and away the most common misconception that I hear about mediation and this is often the reason why many people will not even consider mediating their divorce. Again, the myth is far from reality. The first issue in any case is what exactly is fair? I am almost certain that you and your spouse both have firm ideas as to what you think is fair and I am also sure that you both have different views on what that looks like. The same goes for the court. What the law provides for is often nowhere near what is fair in your mind but that is what a judge must follow. The most common thing I would hear from a client after we got a ruling from a judge is "but that's not fair!" It may not be fair, but in a courtroom, that is what you are stuck with.

In mediation, you and your spouse are free to craft a settlement that feels as close to fair as possible to you both. Remember, there is no agreement until you both agree so there will need to be compromise to get to agreement but again, you are the ones determining what is in the realm of your definition of fair. It is important that you both understand the law around the issues of your divorce, and your mediator will help you by giving you a neutral understanding of the laws, but again, you are free to agree to vary from what the law provides if that is what works best for you both. So, in fact, settlements reached in mediation are most often the ones that are closest to what you think is a fair settlement.

What are some common misconceptions divorcing couples have about mediating a divorce or the family law industry in general?

Susan Guthrie: There is one caution that I have given to almost every client over the years, and that is, if you are looking for justice for your hurt and anger in a courtroom you are not likely to find it there. I think that all clients have some fantasy in their head that in court, a judge will listen to their tale and agree with everything that they are saying and will in some way punish the other person for their bad behavior. This has been the stated reason why many people decide not to mediate their divorce: they don't want to settle, they want JUSTICE! Unfortunately, that is very unlikely to happen in a courtroom. Judges are not moral arbiters and they generally do not take the things that you think are so egregious into consideration when they apply the law to the facts of your case. Keep in mind, every state has a "no fault" divorce law in place and while there are some instances where the judge can consider bad behavior, it is only in cases that are extraordinary. In other words, those cases where the level of bad behavior is so bad that it "shocks the judicial conscience". You have to remember though, that those judges sit there day in and day out listening to all the bad things that people do when their marriages are ending, and it is a long list. The bad behavior of your spouse has to rise to such a level that it is far above what they hear every day, and, in most cases, it will not have an impact on the final judgment. That means that in those cases, people who choose to litigate because they are seeking justice only get caught up in the time, expense and stress of litigation without any of the upsides of mediation and without receiving that justice they were seeking.

What are some of the most common fears about mediating a divorce?

Susan Guthrie: *Beyond their ability?* Many people are concerned that they cannot mediate because they don't know the law or they are not a skilled negotiator and while these are normal concerns, they are both things that the mediation process is well equipped to deal with. First, if you needed to have a complete understanding of the law of divorce in order to mediate, then only attorneys would be able to mediate their divorces. In fact, it is the role of your mediator, who often is an attorney or who has training in the law of divorce, to provide you both with a neutral understanding of all of the legal points that you need to be aware of as you work through your issues. In addition, many people will also have a consulting attorney while they go through mediation. The attorney does not usually attend the sessions but can meet with the client in between sessions to answer any specific legal questions that they may have and to give the client direct legal advice. The parties in mediation are supported in a variety of ways with information on the law so that they can make informed decisions. In addition, no particular skill as a negotiator is needed in mediation. Your mediator is there to help you facilitate your conversations with your ex and will lead you through a process of suggestions, offers and brainstorming to find the right solutions. You are guided through the process. Another very relevant fact is that the person you are negotiating with is your spouse who most people understand better than anyone else. You know what motivates them and what will incentivize them to come to agreements that are important to you. The negotiation process naturally unfolds in mediation and no special skill is necessary.

What if it doesn't work? In the event that you mediate but for some reason one or both of you decides to terminate the process, then the litigation route is always open to you. As I have said before, mediation is entirely voluntary so if you want out you do not have to continue the process. This rarely happens in my experience, but when it does, the couple often has much of the discovery completed and have some agreements in place that they can carry forward into the litigation process so the mediation may still be partially successful. There is little to nothing to lose by attempting to mediate.

What will others think? For the most part, the public perception of mediation is a positive one and families and friends are supportive of a couple attempting to amicably resolve their divorce. When third parties are against using mediation, it is usually because they share the misconceptions about mediation that I discussed above and with the proper understanding of mediation and the many benefits, their opposition will turn to support. In addition, it is very important to note that while the support of family and friends is wonderful to have when you are going through divorce, you must remember that it is your divorce and no one else's. You need to make choices, including whether to mediate, that work for you and your children and not anyone else.

***What are some of the little-known pitfalls or
common mistakes you see divorcing couples
make on the road to mediating a divorce?***

Susan Guthrie: There are a few common mistakes
that I see divorcing couples make while mediating their
divorce. Notably, in an effort to save money, the parties
will decide not to retain a neutral expert when there are
issues that arise that would best be informed by an
outside party with expertise in the area. Some
examples of this are when there is a closely held
business or a house with a value that the parties are
unable to agree upon. It is often best to hire a neutral
evaluator to determine the value of the business so that
there is a consensus based upon facts. Another
example would be where parents are unable to agree on
an aspect of the parenting plan and the effects on their
children of certain proposed schedules. In those cases,
it is often very helpful to have a neutral child therapist
or expert collaborate in the process to inform the
parents on developmental stages of the children and
the impact of the proposed parenting plans on them.
When there are stalemates on the facts, it becomes
impossible to move forward with any agreements
because the parties are both operating from a different
basis. I had a case once where the parties owned a
rather unusual house and they both had very different
views on the value. The husband thought the home was
worth approximately $1,000,000 while the wife felt
that there were special features that made it worth
about twice that. They refused to spend the money,
which would likely have been under $1,000 to have the
property appraised by a jointly agreed upon appraiser
so we hit a major bump in the road that almost derailed
the mediation. They could not reach any agreement on
either of them buying out the other since they were so

far apart on the value. In the end, they agreed to sell the house, so the issue resolved itself, but it did prolong the mediation process by several months while they went back and forth with no progress and they spent more on those sessions than the cost of the appraisal. (For those of you who were wondering about the actual value of that home, it sold for $1,250,000).

Although a major motivating factor in choosing mediation is often to save money, do not be penny wise and pound foolish. In litigation you would usually each be hiring an expert and then would have to argue about who's expert is correct since they rarely agree. In mediation, you will agree upon one expert to use and you will have one neutral evaluation or expert opinion to work with and you will streamline your process and keep your costs down by investing in the help that you need.

Another big mistake that people make in mediation is that they fail to do any of the legwork outside of the sessions or to properly prepare to come to the table and have meaningful discussions. Because you and your spouse are the ones making all the decisions in your divorce, it is very important that you take control of your process. You need to think about what the future looks like for you and what will work for you in that future. In the mediation sessions, many possible solutions to an issue may be discussed without a final decision. Your job, before you come to the next session, is to think about what you would like to see happen and how you would like to tweak the proposal. If you come ready to make agreements, they will get made. If you don't think about it or do any preparation in between sessions, your process will drag out much like it does when you fail to get the outside help that might be needed.

By far the biggest mistake that I see is when clients allow their emotions to rule their decision making. Face it, the emotions that occur when getting divorced are usually the worst ones we can have. Fear, hurt, anger and sadness are difficult to deal with one at a time and they are all usually present as you separate from your spouse. When these emotions are driving you, your decisions are not well reasoned or thought out and this very often leads to either delay and distress or poor decisions being made. Over and over I have seen people get upset while discussing the issues of their divorce and become unreasonable in their demands. This is truly not helpful to either one of you as this will also drag out the process and can even drive you further apart. It is important to do what you can to manage your emotions while you are in this process. These difficult emotions are temporary, and you want to make decisions that are long-lasting and that work for everyone involved. Do not let them derail your process.

How can these pitfalls / mistakes be avoided?

Susan Guthrie: The best way to avoid the first two mistakes is to listen to your mediator when they suggest finding support or help and when needed, build the proper support team so that you are empowered to make the decisions that will stand you and your family in good stead in the years to come. You are paying your mediator for the skill and expertise so allow yourself to be guided when appropriate.

As to the issue of managing your emotions, we strongly believe in getting help because it can be so difficult to do. To that end, at Breaking Free Mediation, we have partnered with one of the leading mindfulness and energy healing experts in the country, Scott Picard, to create the first of its kind, optional mindfulness track for our mediation clients. The mindfulness track offers special one-on-one coaching as well as downloadable tools to help you find some space and peace in the middle of turmoil. In addition, we have incorporated mindfulness techniques, such as intention setting and awareness, right into the mediation process itself. Our success in helping clients through the use of mindfulness has been extraordinary and clients report a much calmer and amicable experience and even more satisfaction with their agreements than even in a regularly mediated case.

Can you share an example of how you have helped your clients overcome these obstacles and succeed in mediating a divorce?

Susan Guthrie: We recently had a couple come to Breaking Free Mediation that had some very unpleasant experiences between them as they decided to divorce. Because there was so much tension and anger in their case, they decided to add the optional mindfulness track to their mediation package. As a part of their first session, we started by asking them both to explain why they chose mediation and what they hoped to achieve through the process. It was a great start as they both said that they wanted a reasonable and fair settlement and most importantly, they wanted to shield their children from any further upheaval and to create a parenting plan that worked best for them. We had our first agreement of the mediation! The most powerful part of this intention setting came later in the mediation, however. Each time the couple would fall back on anger and blame as they discussed things, we would bring them back to their intentions set in that first meeting. It was remarkable how effective that was in drawing them both out of the hurt of the past and helping them to focus on what was important in their, and their children's, future. This divorce actually moved quite quickly, and this couple is very successfully co-parenting their children in post-divorce life.

What's the most important question divorcing couples should ask themselves as they consider mediating a divorce?

Susan Guthrie: Ask yourself what your peace of mind is worth and what it would mean to have the divorce and separation behind you so that you can move forward into your new life, then choose the method that is most likely to get you there. Remember that mediation is almost always less time-consuming, stressful and expensive than a traditional litigated divorce. Be sure to consider mediation when looking at your options.

What's the most important thing divorcing couples should consider when evaluating an attorney and mediator?

Susan Guthrie: Once you decide to mediate, it is very important to find the right mediator. I always suggest interviewing more than one so that you can find someone you both have trust in and feel comfortable with. Get suggestions from friends and family who have mediated or do your research online. There are amazing resources like Divorceify.com, HelloDivorce.com and my website divorceinabetterway.com out there that have lists of resources and mediators that can help you.

It is also important to find a mediator whose process and personal style suit your situation. If you have a high conflict situation, find someone who has experience dealing with that dynamic. As I mentioned, at Breaking Free Mediation both my partner and I were long time litigators dealing with high conflict cases so certainly an attorney/mediator with experience in that area is helpful. If you have complicated finances, perhaps consider a mediator who has experience with your type of matter or who collaborates with a respected financial professional.

Another consideration if you are afraid or uncomfortable being in the same room with your spouse or are just geographically in different places or have issues with traffic and childcare, is online mediation. At Breaking Free Mediation, we offer a fully online mediation service where the parties and their mediator, as well as any of our preferred collaborating professionals all meet via videoconferencing. This allows you to work through the issues of your divorce in the privacy and comfort of your home, office or other secure location, can greatly lessen the time needed for commuting and makes scheduling much easier. As an online mediation expert, I even train other mediators in the implementation of an online platform as this convenience becomes more and more requested by clients.

Always remember that one of the first decisions that you and your spouse must make, after you decide to mediate, is who to use as a mediator so educate yourselves and do your homework. The professional you choose will be your guide through the divorce process and will help you to get to the other side.

How can someone find out more about Susan Guthrie, Esq. and Breaking Free Mediation and how you can help?

Susan Guthrie: If you would like to find out more about me or Breaking Free Mediation's services, please visit our website www.breakingfreemediation.com. We have a great deal of information on the site as well as descriptions of our various mediation packages, including the mindfulness track, as well as our coaching programs.

I also encourage you to listen to our podcast, Breaking Free: A Modern Divorce Podcast (www.breakingfreepod.com) where we interview some of the top experts in divorce and every related field, as well as share our many years of experience and insights on every subject related to divorce, transformation and thriving after divorce.

Finally, as it is so important to educate yourself, I urge you to visit my website, www.divorceinabetterway.com where I have created a curated collection of tips, information and resources to help you navigate divorce.

It is my mission and goal to guide people through the process and divorce in a better way so that they can move on to their future. Please contact me if I can support you.

SUSAN GUTHRIE, ESQ.

Family Law Attorney & Mediator

Founder & Principal, Divorce in a Better Way, Inc.

Susan Guthrie, named by Lawyers of Distinction as one of the Top Family Law and Mediation Attorneys in the country, has been helping individuals and families navigate separation and divorce for 30 years first, as a leading family law litigator specializing in high conflict and high net worth divorces and now, as one of the preeminent family law mediators in the country. Susan is admitted to practice before the bars of the States of California and Connecticut as well as the Supreme Court of the United States of America and mediates nationwide.

As a leading dispute resolution professional, Susan is proud to be a Co-Chair of the American Bar Association's (ABA's) Mediation Committee. Susan also serves the ABA as a Co-Chair of the Planning Committee for the ABA's Advanced Mediation Skills Institute, as an editor of the ABA DR Section Mediation Committee's edition of the e-magazine, "Just Resolutions" and as the Outreach Chair for the Section's podcast: *Resolutions: A Podcast About Dispute Resolution and Prevention*. In addition to her roles with the ABA, Susan is honored to serve on the Board of Directors of the Southern California Mediation Association (SCMA) and is the Co-Chair of the SCMA Communications/Membership Committee. Susan is regularly published in industry and divorce resources and magazines and presents several times a year at conferences and institutes around the country. She is a contributing author to the book "Divorce Insights" which will be available on Amazon in Paperback and Kindle formats as well as through her website www.divorceinabetterway.com.

Susan and fellow top attorney, Rebecca Zung, are the Co-Founders of Breaking Free Mediation (www.breakingfreemediation.com), the first family law mediation service in the country to offer a mindfulness track to help divorcing parties to negotiate their issues peacefully. Breaking Free Mediation offers online mediation services and legal coaching, including high conflict divorce coaching, nationwide through the use of an online platform.

Susan is also the co-host, with Rebecca, of the iTunes Top 10 podcast, *Breaking Free: A Modern Divorce Podcast* (www.breakingfreepod.com), which is revolutionizing the conversation around divorce. The podcast has appeared several times in the iTunes Top Ten and was recently featured in the "New & Noteworthy" listings. Podbean regularly features the show on its "Recommended" list. The show recently reached 1,300,000 downloads in its first year.

Building on the enormous success of the podcast, Susan and Rebecca have teamed with fellow leading attorney Gabrielle Hartley, author of the best-selling book "Better Apart: The Radically Positive Way to Separate" to create a series of empowering divorce retreats for women and men to be held around the country. The Best You Ever (BYE) Divorce Retreats feature a stellar list of experts who help attendees make the mental pivot necessary to transition through divorce, to transform and to thrive on the other side. More information can be found at www.byedivorce.com.

As a Divorce Innovation Specialist, Susan founded Divorce in a Better Way, Inc. (www.divorceinabetterway.com) as a curated resource for those seeking the latest tips, advice and resources for navigating the divorce process smoothly. In addition, with a fully online divorce mediation and legal coaching practice, Susan is an online mediation expert and trains other mediators and professionals in the practical and ethical implementation of an online platform into their existing practice through her business Learn to Mediate Online (www.learntomediateonline.com).

WEBSITE: www.divorceinabetterway.com

EMAIL: susan@divorceinabetterway.com

INSTAGRAM:

https://www.instagram.com/susan_guthrie_esq/

FACEBOOK:

https://www.facebook.com/susaneguthrieesq/

TWITTER: https://twitter.com/guthrielaw

YOUTUBE:

https://www.youtube.com/channel/UCz6xwbpnmnY7

dCq54RQDaqg

OFFICE: 203-295-3388

BETH WIBERG BARBOSA

Your Future on the Line: How to Hire the Right Divorce Attorney

Conversation with Beth Wiberg Barbosa

Tell us a little bit about yourself, Gilbert Alden Barbosa PLLC, and the type of clients that you serve:

Beth Wiberg Barbosa: I have been practicing family law for over 20 years. Over the years I have refined my practice to serving clients with complex cases involving high marital assets, business ownership and professional practices. There is a financial complexity to these cases that often includes issues such as business valuation, stock options, executive compensation packages, commercial real estate appraisals, retirement accounts, spousal maintenance, child custody and child support.

It is important to understand that not all assets are created equal, which I believe many family law attorneys do not know. Because of the tax consequences, it is extremely important to divide pre-tax assets separate from post-tax assets. Understanding these complexities are important when I work with my clients because it can impact the overall results my clients achieve in the division of marital assets and debts, as well as in custody and spousal and/or child support. Each client has a different goal in and understanding of their expectations. Acknowledging this is paramount when I strategize a plan to achieve a resolution whether it is through mediation or litigation. A resolution through mediation is always better for clients because they have control over the agreement reached and it allows the parties to think outside of the box to be creative in resolving the issues that will be fair and equitable to both parties and their respective goals. In addition, mediation is far less costly than litigation. I am in practice to help my clients settle their cases, not to encourage litigation in all cases. There are times when mediation doesn't work. In those unique situations, I am prepared to zealously advocate on behalf of my clients in front of a judge.

One of the biggest strengths I bring to clients is my knowledge and mastery of complex financial situations, and how to negotiate the best settlement for clients who have a lot to lose if they do not work with an attorney who has demonstrated experience working with business executives, business owners and medical professionals. It's clear these types of clients all have a lot to lose if their divorce attorney does not have high level financial analysis experience.

What is the number one worry you hear from your clients when you first meet?

Beth Wiberg Barbosa: I think the number one worry for all of my clients is their financial well-being after the divorce proceeding. All my clients are used to a certain standard of living - generally higher than average - and whether both parties worked or only one party worked, their marital standard of living will be affected by the divorce. It doesn't matter whether a client has a marital estate less than $500,000 or $5 million. The marital estate will be divided, and my client will have less assets and less income to support their marital standard of living than they had pre-divorce. Just by the nature of a divorce and the stress it can cause, too often my clients are only able to think about the immediate needs and fail to think about their long-term goals. As a result, I have developed and implemented an intake form that specifically seeks to uncover the specific five goals they have after the divorce is finalized. I have found this to be an extremely important tool when I advise and strategize with my clients on negotiating a property distribution, custody, spousal maintenance, as well as separating non-marital assets from the asset pool.

What do you feel are the biggest myths out there when it comes to the divorce process?

Beth Wiberg Barbosa: As I work with my clients, I realize there are a lot of misconceptions out there about the divorce process overall. Some of the most common myths I've found include:

Myth: Getting a divorce can be a fast process.
Truth: Generally, it is not. It can be a longer process, spanning months to, in some cases, years. The court system is not set up to be reactive. If you want a court hearing, you are likely looking at 2-3 months to get in front of the judge because of their packed schedules.

Myth: Antenuptial Agreements will be upheld in Court.
Truth: The law is changing. I'm finding that Antenuptial Agreements are being questioned more by the court. In general, the court will determine whether the agreement is substantively fair.

Myth: I have to learn to fight dirty if I want my way in the divorce.
Truth: This will only protract your divorce. If the court thinks you are not being honest, it could negatively affect your custody arrangements and financial settlement. You could even be hit with "conduct-based attorney's fees," for any bad behavior demonstrated.

Myth: I need an aggressive, litigious lawyer if I want to win.
Truth: You want an experienced family lawyer who approaches the process with a settlement mindset, not a litigation-only mindset. Litigation is expensive and generally is only necessary in about 5% of all divorce cases.

Myth: If I hide my assets, no one will be the wiser.

Truth: This is illegal, and you will be held to account for any deception you try to implement. If the court finds out later there were hidden assets, the court can reopen the Judgment and Decree, which will result in additional cost to you.

What are some common misconceptions surrounding divorce or the family law industry in general?

Beth Wiberg Barbosa: Many clients believe that going to trial and "fighting it out in court" is the only answer to resolving a case. However, I would say that 99% of all cases should be resolved in mediation without having to air a client's dirty laundry in court. I strongly believe that mediation produces better settlements than trial because both parties have control over the outcome.

Many people believe that if they have their day in Court, justice will prevail. This is truly a misconception and one that I try to educate my clients on at the beginning. A judge makes a decision based upon a two- or three-day trial after hearing witnesses and receiving evidence. However, at the end of the day, a judge is persuaded by his or her own biases and beliefs when he/she makes a decision. I had a recent case where my client and I believed we had concrete evidence to disprove the custody evaluator's report including detailed medical records and therapy notes and experts including psychological evaluations. The Court ignored the concrete evidence because of his own personal biases against my client. He simply did not like him, which was evidenced by comments about my client's demeanor in court. As a result, the judge issued an order that went against my client. I believe it was the wrong decision because the Court ignored concrete evidence to support my client's claim. And, we will be back before the judge within a year because of the wife's mental health issues. My client could not believe the judge ignored all of the evidence that we presented at trial. This was not justice. This is a good example of how justice doesn't always prevail.

What are some of the most common fears about the divorce process?

Beth Wiberg Barbosa: A lot of clients are divorcing for the first time. Naturally, fear of the unknown is very real for them. I try to ease their fear by walking through the divorce process and the various steps involved, allowing them to ask as many questions as they have. I really try to understand my client's goals and accomplish this through inquiring about where they would like to see themselves five years after their divorce. A good example is that many clients want to keep the family home often times for the children and/or sentimental value. I will have an honest discussion with my clients about the pros and cons of keeping the marital home. Many times, it may not be financially feasible or smart to keep the marital home. Leaving the marital home causes a lot of fear for some clients. The number one fear associated with leaving the marital homestead is the emotional impact it will have on the children. When this occurs, I will discuss that fear with them and try to come up with solutions to resolve their fear. Sometimes, I will refer them to a therapist to help work through their own emotional guilt associated with letting their children down if they move from the marital home.

The idea of co-parenting with a spouse can also cause fear for a client because of relationship issues such as mental health or inability to communicate effectively. I have found a good resource is referring my clients to private parenting coaches to learn how to communicate and co-parent with their spouses and most importantly to learn to set boundaries. It's really about operating in ways that place the emotional health of the children as a top priority.

What are some of the little-known pitfalls or common mistakes you see people make during the divorce process?

Beth Wiberg Barbosa: There are a number of pitfalls and mistakes I have seen clients make over the years including:

Being Honest - Honesty with your attorney is extremely important. Often, I tell clients that my advice and strategy is only as good as the information they provide to me. Being blindsided by important information can negatively affect a case. I cannot stress this enough. I would rather know negative information ahead of time because I can then determine the best way to handle the information.

Disclosing All Assets and Debts - Some clients have the "Swiss bank account" mentality and think they can choose to not disclose material assets they have. Disclosing every single asset and debt is critically important to my ability to help negotiate a fair and just divorce settlement.

Emotional Decision Making - Another mistake I have found some clients make is that they make decisions based on emotions, which do not produce good agreements. Because I represent a lot of business owners, I tell them that a divorce is at its core a business transaction. When I believe a decision is being made solely based upon emotion, I will ask them to analyze the same issue as though they were in a boardroom. I call it my "Boardroom Test." More often than not, they will admit that the decision would be a poor decision. I find that this a good and respectful way to allow them to reach a better decision because they can relate to making a "business decision."

Using the Children - Another pitfall that I see are clients involving their children in the divorce proceeding by talking about the specifics and/or saying negative things about the other parent. I remind my clients that their children are comprised of one-half of the genetics of their spouse. To say anything negative about their spouse to their children is directly saying something negative about the children. I remind my clients that just because they are divorcing their spouse, doesn't mean they are also divorcing their children. There will be big events such as graduations, weddings and grandchildren. Therefore, they need to be cordial so that they can be involved in these big events. I have had clients who have told me that there was so much animosity that their children did not invite them to these big events. I tell clients to avoid being placed in that position by treating their spouse with respect, and acknowledging the important role both parents play in the lives of their children. Children will always figure out each parent's flaws; parents do not have to tell them. I may refer clients to a therapist or to a parenting coach to help them work through their issues and to effectively co-parent not just now, but through the years ahead.

Can you share an example of a difficult divorce case and how you created the best possible outcome?

Beth Wiberg Barbosa: Following are a few examples of the types of clients I have assisted:

Chief Executive Officer – I represented the CEO of a land development business in his divorce where a major sticking point was the value of his business. I retained an appraiser knowledgeable in land development who found that the business as it existed at the time had little to no value. We also retained a financial neutral. As a result of this collaboration, we negotiated a settlement in which my client paid no maintenance to his former spouse.

Physician – We represented a doctor in a divorce matter where there was a potential claim for spousal maintenance. The wife had supported my client through medical school and his residency period and was requesting spousal maintenance. We negotiated a settlement where my client did not pay ongoing spousal maintenance.

Business Partner – In this case, I represented the wife of the owner of a closely held business. At issue was the need to establish a fair buyout price of the business as well as a determination of ongoing spousal maintenance. We retained a business appraiser to determine the value of the company as well as a financial neutral who performed a cash flow analysis. As a result, we were able to engage in mediation, successfully negotiating a buyout of the business and an award of spousal maintenance.

Corporate Vice President – A retired corporate vice president retained me in a divorce matter where he faced potential exposure to on ongoing spousal maintenance obligation. I negotiated a multimillion-dollar property settlement that eliminated the need for my client to pay ongoing spousal maintenance to his ex-wife.

Physician – One physician I represented in his divorce was concerned about whether the value of his practice may obligate him to pay high monthly spousal maintenance to his ex. Working with other professionals, I was able to estimate his practice's value. I did this by retaining a neutral appraiser to value the business side of his practice, and a financial neutral to provide a three-year spending analysis. The data we collected from these professionals showed that my client's wife's request for spousal maintenance was too high. As a result, we negotiated a maintenance buyout and property settlement. This allowed my physician client to maintain his business without interference from his ex-spouse.

Nurse Anesthetist - I represented a Certified Registered Nurse Anesthetist, whose husband was claiming spousal maintenance and a division of his outstanding university loans. We engaged in a mediation process that resulted in no spousal maintenance being owed to the husband and his agreement to take on the full obligation of his student loans. The couple agreed to an equal division of marital debts.

Chief Executive Officer - In another case I worked with a financial industry CEO. His goal was two-fold: to maintain the ownership of his stock, and to avoid a cumbersome level of spousal maintenance. We worked closely with an expert, a financial neutral, who analyzed the current and future value of the stock. He also created an updated cash flow analysis to identify how the stock would payout now and into the future. The result was exactly what my client wanted. We were able to negotiate a lower monthly spousal maintenance payment.

Attorney - It can be challenging when attorneys go through a divorce. Because of the complexity of being part of a partnership, this lawyer was dealing with the big issue of how to preserve my client's interest in the law practice. In addition, we were dealing with complex issues involving spousal maintenance, property division, and allocation of debt acquired during the marriage. My client did not want his ex to have any future interest in the law practice. As always, we attempted mediation first, but that effort failed. At trial, we succeeded on all fronts. First, the court denied the wife's demand of alimony. In addition, the court awarded all of my client's pre-marriage assets and equally split the marriage debt. The best part? The court found that my client was entitled to his entire interest in the law firm.

"You are always willing to go above and beyond to do the best for your clients. You tell the truth no matter what to ensure your clients don't get their hopes up. If I left a message, you answered or called back ASAP and if I was really upset you were right there to talk me through it. You are a very compassionate soul and loving person. You are driven and work hard to get it done right." — L.P., Client

Here is a link to additional feedback I have received from my clients:
https://bethbarbosa.com/#1517435661637-98bf53c2-6b40

What inspired you to get into family law?

Beth Wiberg Barbosa: When I was in my second year of law school, I clerked for the county child support division. I was a student attorney and represented the county in child support modifications before the administrative law judge. I was assisting families in getting child support, which could either make or break a family financially. A lot of these families depended on the child support to help meet their monthly budget. It broke my heart witnessing families be impacted by such a small decrease in child support.

Immediately after law school, I practiced in the area of family probate law for a few years. Both areas of practice focused on assisting families during difficult periods of their lives. My clients come to me when they are in an emotional crisis. Although the divorce rate is still approximately 50%, I don't believe anyone gets married thinking about or planning to get divorced. It doesn't matter whether a client has an average marital estate or a high marital estate, each client is worried about being financially stable after the divorce process.

It is my passion to help my clients negotiate a settlement that will enable them to move confidently into the next chapter of their life. I accomplish this through building an open and trusting relationship with my clients by listening to their concerns, providing straightforward advice, asking them hard questions, learning about their goals and never being judgmental. In return my clients feel comfortable being honest with me; and yes, sometimes they get upset and I receive the brunt of their frustrations. Often times, the relationship with their spouse will continue even into the next chapter of their life. It is the human connection and relationship with my clients that is the foundation of my family law practice.

Can you share a lesson you learned early on, that still impacts how you do business today?

Beth Wiberg Barbosa: I learned early in my practice that being accessible to my clients is important to my business. I give clients my cell phone number and I encourage them to email, call or text should they have a question. I understand that going through a divorce is stressful and questions or concerns come up outside of office hours. I would rather have my client contact me and ask me a question or talk through a concern that often takes less than fifteen minutes than have them stress about it all night (lose sleep) or spend time worrying over a weekend. It is important for my clients to know that I do care about their well-being.

I had a client who decided to retain another attorney because she believed having an attorney where she lived would be more beneficial. However, she did not receive the same level of client service and responsiveness. Her former attorney was hardly ever available and only communicated by email. The attorney certainly was not available outside of office hours. My client grew very frustrated and realized that I provided a level of service that was missing with her new attorney. When emergencies occurred, she would call me because she knew I cared about her well-being. My client rehired me three months later, $23,000 in debt to an attorney and law firm she did not feel was at all responsive to her needs. You can't learn to care about clients in law school. It is an inherent trait that lawyers either genuinely have or they don't. For me, it's part of the essence of who I am as a person.

What is the most important question divorcing couples should ask themselves as they consider beginning the divorce process?

Beth Wiberg Barbosa: I am a strong believer in being proactive. Many times, I have clients that consult with me because they are thinking about starting the divorce process in the next year or so. I advise these clients to obtain and copy as many financial records as possible. It is always easier to obtain the information ahead of time rather than later. Also, it can be costly to obtain during the divorce process through discovery. I believe this gives my clients a good understanding of their assets, debts and family monthly budget, which will be extremely helpful in the divorce process and negotiating a settlement or at trial. Clients should start to determine what their goals are after the divorce proceeding. These goals will help create a roadmap of which assets to negotiate for in settlement discussions.

Clients simply want to know that they will be ok after the divorce is finalized. They want to know that they will be financially stable, and able to move with confidence into the next phase of their lives.

I believe clients need to ask themselves if divorce is the right solution for them, their children, and their family unit. Many times, there are situations where two people who previously loved each other grow apart. Their lives move in different directions and they come to a conclusion that divorce is the answer. There really are situations where marriage counseling can help a couple determine if divorce is the right path of action, or if there is a possibility of reconciliation. When I work with people who aren't quite sure about filing for divorce, we also talk about other strategies including counseling, couples' therapy, and other visualization and goal-setting exercises that will confirm their decision that divorce is the answer.

What's the most important thing divorcing couples should consider when evaluating a divorce professional?

Beth Wiberg Barbosa: In addition to experience, I tell potential clients how critical it is that they feel comfortable with the attorney they hire. By and large, divorce lawyers with experience will be able to handle your divorce. That said, divorces can go on for months, and in large complex cases, years. The initial consultation provides a great opportunity for you to interview the lawyer, and for the lawyer to interview you. Just like any relationship, there needs to be a personality match. You must like, trust, and respect the lawyer you are meeting with, and they should, through their actions and questions, show you they feel the same way.

Clients are going to invest a lot of money in a divorce proceeding so it's important they deeply trust the attorney they select to advocate for them. It is important that the lines of communication remain open on both sides. I give honest advice to my clients, which sometimes, they may not want to hear. I know the law and many times they are very emotional psychologically. The great thing about being a lawyer is that I can make the recommendations I believe are right, but in the end, it is always the client's decision on how to proceed.

Another thing clients need to be wary of is that certain family law lawyers actively move their client toward litigation. They are not "settlement-oriented" lawyers. If a lawyer pushes and pushes for a trial, the client will generally take their advice. What clients don't realize is that by going to trial in a divorce case, they will need to air their dirty laundry in front of a courtroom full of people, and give up their rights to the judge who will impartially listen to both sides and make a ruling. Litigation is also extremely expensive. Depending upon the size of the marital estate, high asset divorces can generate over $1 million in fees for the lawyer. Yes, there are times when litigation is necessary, but only when all other forms of mediation and settlement discussions have failed. Litigation should be viewed as the "last resort" in a family law case. That said, many family lawyers know the cost of litigation and move their clients in that direction anyway. Some lawyers do so because it generates income and revenue for them personally, even if it is not in the best interest of the client.

Please know that most lawyers are not litigation pushers. But it's important when meeting with a family lawyer for the first time to ask questions like:

- What is your philosophy on litigation?
- What is your philosophy on mediation?
- How many cases have you personally handled with clients in my situation?
- How do you keep clients informed on the status of their cases?
- How accessible are you to your clients with your busy schedule?
- How much of my case will you handle, versus having your associates and paralegals handle?
- How do you bill for your services, and do you have an estimate for my case as I have described it to you?
- What is your retainer? Note: This is the amount clients pay generally in a lump sum of anywhere from $2,500 to tens of thousands of dollars. Lawyers then work this amount off which requires you to consistently over the course of the divorce proceeding, to replenish the retainer.

I recommend you interview at least three lawyers knowing some will do free consultations and others, you may need to pay for their time. Remember you are interviewing the lawyer, but they are also interviewing you. Lawyers want to know that you can be counted on to provide documents the lawyer requests, and to actively engage in your own divorce.

Choosing the right lawyer will impact and inform the experience you have throughout the divorce process. Assuming all of the lawyers you meet with will be qualified to handle your case, you need to hire someone you personally connect with, who is caring and compassionate, while at the same time, ready to zealously advocate for what you want out of the divorce.

How can someone find out more about you and how can they get your help?

Beth Wiberg Barbosa: If you would like to learn more about me, go to my website: https://www.bethbarbosa.com, email me at bbarbosa@gilbertalden.com or call me at 612-564-0137. I also publish a blog with a lot of useful information for those contemplating divorce at https://bethbarbosa.com/family-law-blog/. You can also visit this page, https://bethbarbosa.com/services/ to review a menu of services I provide, or find a summary of the types of clients for whom I work at https://bethbarbosa.com/clients/.

BETH WIBERG BARBOSA, ESQ.

Partner, Family Law

Gilbert Alden Barbosa, PLLC

Beth is pleased to offer her clients a wealth of experience gained over 20 years of working with many high-profile, high asset, financially complex cases. One of the aspects of her practice that she enjoys most is dealing with the financial issues inherent with clients who own businesses, have executive compensation packages, or are members of a professional association including physicians, attorneys, financial professionals and many other types of professional services. Over the years, Beth has built a solid network of experts required in complex divorce matters including business valuation experts, financial neutrals, independent business appraisers, real estate valuation experts, parenting coaches and more. She also enjoys representing clients on a host of other family law matters including the development of pre-nuptial agreements, post-decree modifications, custody, child support, and parenting time.

Beth earned her law degree in 1998 from William Mitchell College of Law and completed her undergraduate degree in Political Science from Gustavus Adolphus College in St. Peter, Minnesota.

MEMBERSHIPS & BAR ADMISSIONS
- Admitted to the Minnesota Bar Association, 2002
- Admitted to the United States District Court for the District of Minnesota, 2011
- Admitted to the Connecticut Bar Association, 1999
- Member - Minnesota State Bar Association
- Member - Hennepin County Bar Association Fourth District Ethics Committee
- Member - Ramsey County Bar Association
- Member - Minnesota Asian Pacific American Bar Association
- Graduate - Harvard Negotiation Institute, Harvard University, 2012
- Certified - Qualified Neutral under Rule 114 of the Minnesota General Rules of Practice
- Trained Parenting Time Expeditor
- Member - Family Law Form Committee, Minnesota State Bar Association

WEBSITE: https://www.bethbarbosa.com

EMAIL: bbarbosa@gilbertalden.com

LINKEDIN:

https://www.linkedin.com/in/bethbarbosa

FACEBOOK: https://www.facebook.com/Beth-

Barbosa

OFFICE: 612-564-0137

JOSEPH F. EMMERTH IV

How to Avoid Common Mistakes During a Divorce

Conversation with Joseph Emmerth

Tell us a little bit about yourself, STG Law Firm, and the type of clients that you serve:

Joseph Emmerth: Founded in 1994, Sullivan Taylor and Gumina is one of the largest law firms in Illinois specializing in family and matrimonial law. We help men and women prepare for divorce, navigate the divorce process, and complete the divorce while maintaining their dignity and financial well-being. We also deal with other family law issues such as adoptions, surrogacy and alternative reproduction technologies, parentage cases, and prenuptial and postnuptial agreements.

Although I represent both men and women in divorce cases, most of my caseload is dedicated to representing men in the divorce process. There are several other attorneys in the area who claim to be champions for "father's rights", or "attorneys for fathers", but unfortunately most of these attorneys treat their clients like ATMs. They charge a huge upfront retainer, blow through it quickly, and then withdraw from the case leaving their clients high and dry. I specialize in helping men navigate the divorce process, fighting back against a system rigged in women's favor, and getting them the results and the outcomes that they deserve. I wrote an entire book on helping divorcing men entitled "Winning Your Divorce: The Top Ten Mistakes Men Make And How To Avoid Them."

Most men are terrified that they are going to be financially ruined as a result of the divorce, or that they won't get to be involved in the lives of the children in the same capacity. I help men protect their financial assets so that they can emerge from the divorce with a solid financial footing and a financial plan. I ensure that my clients get the time they need to be a dad and father to their children, and not merely some weekend visitor.

Helping men to avoid getting abused by the court system is the most rewarding aspect of my career. Seeing the relief on my client's faces when they realize their spouse is not going to be taking them to the proverbial "cleaners" financially is priceless. Ensuring that my clients have a stable financial footing post-divorce that they can build on and live a rewarding life with gives them hope and confidence for the future. The joy of knowing that they will continue to be a frequent and integral part of their children's upbringing and development reaffirms their role as a dad and father, not just in their own lives, but in their community and society at large.

What are the advantages of choosing to work with you?

Joseph Emmerth: Working with me gives my clients many advantages over the average divorce attorney. Number one, at my law firm we work on a team system. Every case gets assigned a partner, an associate, and a paralegal. This means that there will always be someone in the office who can answer their questions and give them the information that they need, even if a member of the team is at court, in a deposition, or on vacation.

Secondly, my background in counseling allows me to better understand and better navigate the often contentious and adversarial emotions and behavior that manifest during the typical divorce process. By maintaining a calm, objective, and unwavering dedication to our plan, I am able to avoid getting caught in common pitfalls and traps set by opposing counsel and/or their client.

Lastly, I practice solely in the field of family and matrimonial law. I don't do criminal law on the side, nor do I take personal injury cases or other unrelated matters. I pride myself on devoting all my focus to this specialty for the past fifteen years. There is a reason that my peers have voted me an Illinois Superlawyer and Leading Lawyer over and over again. My clients benefit from that experience and expertise.

What do you feel is one of the biggest myths out there when it comes to the divorce process?

Joseph Emmerth: One of the biggest myths that men fall prey to is that they should move out of the house at the beginning of the divorce. This is the biggest myth and the biggest mistake that I see men making in their divorces. While remaining in the same house during the divorce may be uncomfortable, it is precisely that uncomfortable environment that encourages both parties to operate in good faith and work towards an equitable resolution. By moving out of the home, men usually guarantee that they will see their children less and increase their financial obligations, since they will now have two households to pay for each month. Moving out can also backfire in a huge way. Think about it, you may be giving your soon to be ex-wife exactly what she wants: her normal life, financed by you, but without you in it. Very few women in that position have any incentive to bring the divorce to an efficient conclusion.

Another myth that men tend to believe is that they need to immediately start setting up their new, post-divorce life. Many men will start doing unnecessary things, such as buying a new home or condo, immediately starting a new romantic relationship with someone, or attempting to cut off their soon-to-be ex-wife from all of the financial accounts. These are all huge mistakes. You don't want to start creating new assets before the divorce is over, or you may be forced to divide those as well. You also don't want to jump into a new relationship immediately. Give yourself some time to heal and adjust to your new life. And nothing throws gasoline on a divorce fire like cutting off the other spouse from the finances. Doing that usually results in immediate action against you by the court and ratchets up the animosity to level ten. This results in a much more expensive and lengthy divorce process.

What are some common misconceptions surrounding divorce or the family law industry in general?

Joseph Emmerth: One of the most common misconceptions is that both sides don't need an attorney. Many men think that, since they and their soon-to-be ex-wife agree on just about everything, it will be okay if they simply use their wife's attorney to "draw up the papers." Let me be clear: this is an awful idea. Your wife's attorney has one person's best interests in mind, and it's not yours. Many men have been steamrolled by their wife's attorney without even knowing it was happening. You need your own independent legal counsel to give you the advice that is in your best interests, and to prevent the other attorney from slipping things into the paperwork that you are completely unaware are being included.

Another common misconception is that you will be perfectly fine representing yourself in court. Many men figure it will be cheaper than hiring an attorney if they just represent themselves. While it's true that they will "save" money by not paying a retainer, the end result is always more costly for the man, as they lack the experience and the technical knowledge to fight for a fair settlement, or even know what a fair settlement looks like. We already know the courts are biased against men in divorce cases. Why would you walk into an environment where everyone is an expert except for you? Do you really think it will be a level playing field? Do you really think that's a good idea? Do yourself a favor and hire your own attorney.

What are some of the most common fears about the divorce process?

Joseph Emmerth: Most men are afraid that they will be financially ruined by their spouse in a divorce. Another common fear is that their children will be "taken away from them", and that they will hardly ever see them. Older men often fear that they won't be able to retire, or that they will have to retire much, much later than they had planned as a result of the divorce. Still other men fear that they will lose standing or status in their social circles or in their community, or even worse, have to find new social circles or new communities in which to start over.

How can potential clients get past these fears??

Joseph Emmerth: The quickest and best way to get past these fears is to immediately schedule a consultation with a qualified and respected divorce attorney, one who is experienced and knowledgeable about the law in your unique situation. For instance, during my consultations with prospective clients, we go over the divorce process itself and how it applies to their particular situation. We look at the law, discuss its application to their individual circumstances, and start to formulate a plan for the divorce process that helps them achieve their goals and gets them the results they deserve. 'Fear' is anxiety about the unknown, and it can't survive in an information-rich environment. I give my clients the knowledge and the information they need to make informed decisions, create comprehensive plans, and follow through to achieve their goals.

What other perceived obstacles do you see that might be preventing divorcing couples from seeking the help of a divorce attorney?

Joseph Emmerth: Some divorcing couples feel like they simply can't afford divorce attorneys, or they worry that once attorneys get involved the case is going to drag out for years and years while the attorneys fight. I blame the mass media for this perception. The only time the public is really exposed to the concept of divorce by the mass media is when there are extremely high net worth divorces or celebrity divorces the media wants to sensationalize. This focus on the "1%" divorces skews the general public's perception of how the majority of divorces are really resolved. Only about one in 20 cases actually go to trial. Most cases are done in less than a year. Most divorce attorneys don't drive around in exotic sports cars while lighting their cigars with $100-dollar bills. Most divorce attorneys are regular people, just like their clients.

What are some of the little-known pitfalls or common mistakes you see people make during the divorce process?

Joseph Emmerth: I see a lot of people who are in such a rush to get divorced that they skip several very important steps of the process. Both parties need to fully disclose all their financial assets and debts, but a lot of couples skip this step because they want to get the divorce done as quickly as possible. A lot of couples also fail to include specifics in their divorce documents. Also, because they are rushing through the process, sometimes couples focus on concerns that deal mainly with "here and now" issues, but completely fail to take into account the long-term ramifications of those decisions. Common examples of these things include, but are not limited to: waiving your interest in your spouse's retirement fund; failing to specify how assets are to be divided, or in what percentage; assigning debts in one person's name to the other person; and overlooking or forgetting about certain assets and debts completely.

How can these pitfalls / mistakes be avoided?

Joseph Emmerth: I might be starting to sound like a broken record here but having your own independent legal counsel can prevent you from making these types of mistakes. I realize the prospect of
hiring your own attorney is a financial commitment some divorcing couples don't want to make. However, the cost of retaining your own attorney pales in comparison to the amount of time and money you will spend coming back to court over and over again to correct or modify the documents you initially agreed to. Not to mention, the amount of money you lost (or may have to spend in the future) by failing to include or consider certain assets or the long-term impact of their division (or lack thereof).

Can you share an example of how you have helped a client in a particularly difficult situation overcome these obstacles and succeed in a smooth divorce process?

Joseph Emmerth: I could give you dozens of examples. I had a client who worked a nontraditional schedule, meaning twenty-four hours on and then forty-eight hours off. He had been representing himself throughout the process and the other attorney had been taking advantage of him. He was on the verge of signing a settlement document that was going to give him four overnights per month with his son and lock him into a child support payment of over $800 per month.

Depressed and looking to find some sort of guidance, he scheduled a consultation with me. A quick review of the proposed settlement documents revealed that he was being steamrolled by the other side. I went through the proposed settlement document with him, told him which portions were typical and which portions were not, highlighted the areas where he was being taken advantage of, and then suggested to him what a more equitable settlement would look like. He retained me as his attorney shortly thereafter, at which point I fired off a letter to opposing counsel essentially shredding his settlement proposal and indicating that I was going to set this case for trial and take his client's deposition. Opposing counsel immediately offered to meet with me at his office and discuss more reasonable settlement terms. Subsequent to our settlement meeting, we were able to enter into a settlement agreement that gave my client eight overnights per month, joint decision-making for the minor child, and a child support obligation almost $200 less per month than what was originally proposed. I was also able to convince the judge to reduce their attorney fee award from $9,000 to $2,500. This is only one example of an instance where I was able to bring the client's case to a swift conclusion, while also obtaining a far more favorable parenting arrangement and a much more favorable financial resolution.

What inspired you to become a divorce attorney?

Joseph Emmerth: It was actually an epiphany that I had one day in law school. Divorce law classes are not required in law school, but you can take them as an

elective. I had taken the divorce class taught by an adjunct faculty member who was a practicing divorce attorney in the community. During our second or third class, I remember sitting there when everything "clicked." I realized that I understood the concepts and the rationales behind these laws instinctively. And with my background in counseling, I wasn't going to have any problem dealing with the emotional conflict that accompanies this area of practice. I went on to get the top grade in the class and was later hired by my professor as a clerk in his divorce practice. Many attorneys don't like to practice divorce law because they don't like dealing with the uncomfortable emotions and sometimes irrational behavior of the clients. Because those things don't phase me, and because I'm able to keep an objective viewpoint and my wits about me (even if my client
or the other side cannot) I am able to effectively and efficiently resolve cases and accomplish my client's goals.

What is the most important question divorcing couples should ask themselves?

Joseph Emmerth: They should ask themselves if they want to get divorced in the quickest way possible, and then spend the next ten years coming back to court to deal with the consequences of being
hasty and uninformed? Or, alternatively, would they rather proceed in a calm, organized, and efficient fashion, and arrive at a resolution that is detailed, comprehensive, and expertly crafted so that they don't have to return to court ever again?

What is the most important thing divorcing couples should consider when evaluating a divorce attorney?

Joseph Emmerth: When evaluating a divorce attorney, the most important thing to consider is trust. Do you trust this person sitting across the table from you to advocate for your best interests and to fight for you to achieve your goals? What do his former clients say about him? What do his peers say about him? Does he have a good reputation? Is he being honest with you or is he just telling you what you want to hear? At the end of the day, you need to be able to rely on an attorney who works with you and gives you the information you need to create a plan and a strategy that will accomplish your goals and get you the results that you deserve.

How can someone find out more about Joseph Emmerth and STG Law Firm and how you can help?

Joseph Emmerth: Please visit my website: www.josephemmerth.com, or my firm's website: www.stglawfirm.com. You can also find my book on Amazon, "Winning Your Divorce: The Top Ten Mistakes Men Make and How to Avoid Them." I have a popular video channel on YouTube.com called the "Men's Divorce Minute." You're also welcome to give me a call at my office: 630-665-7676. I look forward to seeing how I can help you!

JOSEPH F. EMMERTH IV, ESQ.

Partner, Family Law

Sullivan Taylor & Gumina, P.C.

Joseph has been voted a Leading Lawyer and an Illinois SuperLawyer by his fellow attorneys since 2015. Admitted to practice law in Illinois in 2005, Joseph graduated from Andrews University, Berrien Springs, MI, where he earned an M.A. in Counseling and was awarded the Nichol Memorial Award for Integrity. Joseph is a graduate of DePaul University College of Law, where he served as a student representative on the Law School's curriculum committee. With several years of experience as a counselor prior to attending law school, Joseph brings unique and valuable experience to the field of Family Law. Joseph is a member of the Illinois State Bar Association, the DuPage County, Kendall County and Will County Bar Associations, and remains active in Phi Alpha Delta Legal Fraternity. Joseph was appointed to the Illinois State Bar Association Committee on Judicial Evaluations and is admitted to practice at the United States Supreme Court. Joseph is a partner at the matrimonial law firm of Sullivan Taylor & Gumina, P.C., with offices in Chicago, Naperville and St. Charles, Illinois. Joseph concentrates his practice in dissolution of marriage matters, prenuptial and postnuptial agreements, and post-divorce modifications.

Joseph also released his first book in 2017, titled "Winning Your Divorce: The Top Ten Mistakes Men Make and How to Avoid Them". You can purchase his book at https://www.amazon.com/dp/1973108844.

WEBSITE: www.stglawfirm.com ,

www.josephemmerth.com

EMAIL: joseph@stglaw.com

LINKEDIN:

https://www.linkedin.com/in/josephemmerth/

TWITTER: www.twitter.com/JosephEmmerth

YOUTUBE:

https://www.youtube.com/user/midnightindustries/featured

OFFICE: 630-665-7676

SHANNON HOLLAND

Empowering Women Through Financial Planning

Conversation with Shannon Holland

Tell us about how you are helping your clients:

Shannon Holland: My typical client is what I refer to as a "financial delegator." This is someone who has been accustomed to delegating all of the financial responsibilities to another party. In most cases, these are divorced or widowed women. Because their spouse was controlling everything, these women are unsure of how much they can spend or where their assets are. This is where I come in. I act as an advocate for these women and become a trusted advisor who guides them on a journey through comprehensive financial planning and independence. I pride myself on helping clients organize their finances in such a way that is in alignment with their most deeply held values and helps them achieve their most important goals.

What does your approach look like when it comes to financial planning for women of divorcing couples?

Shannon Holland: An important step in my process is having a values discussion. I use this to gain clarity about what is important to the client when it comes to money. For example, a client may answer "security". And then I ask, "What is important about security to you?" We continue to walk through a "values staircase" so that the client and I have a very clear understanding of what's important to them and what it will mean to achieve these goals. During the initial conversation, we also take time to make sure their goals align with their values. Sometimes a client gives me a goal that clearly does not align with their values. For example, a client going through a divorce tells me that their goal is to buy an expensive car in three years. Since we have already had their values discussion and discussed other goals that include helping family, becoming a better person, and getting closer to God, I try to understand from the clients perspective, how this goal of purchasing an expensive car is in alignment with what they have told me is most important to them. I am truthful with my clients and a large part of what I do involves keeping them focused on a path that will help lead them to financial stability AND help them achieve their goals in alignment with their most deeply held values.

What are the biggest myths out there regarding the work that you do for women in divorcing couples?

Shannon Holland: One of the biggest myths is that the judicial system is fair when it comes to dealing with divorce. Unfortunately, there is bias when it comes to letting a judge determine your fate during a divorce. You have to consider what his/her life experiences have been and how this will ultimately affect the decision that is essentially being made for you. In my experience, there has not been a great deal of consistency within the judicial system. For example, I've seen a guy making $1 million a year end up paying $2,000 a month in alimony and another guy making $150,000 a year paying $3,500 a month in alimony. There just isn't any rhyme or reason. This could be prevented if attorneys were arming their clients with all options and holding a high standard of fiduciary responsibility to the client. Going to court is not the only option when facing divorce. Mediation, cooperation and collaboration divorces are other viable options.

What are some of the biggest fears that divorcing women come to you with?

Shannon Holland: A universal theme that I see is a husband who is the primary earner truly believing that all the assets belong to him. He worked for 37 years and his wife stayed at home, so she should not be entitled to anything in his eyes. As a result, many divorcing women come into our first meeting very concerned about how they are going to make it on their own. They have questions such as "How am I going to live on this fixed amount of money?" , "Am I going to struggle financially?", "Am I going to be okay, and how can you assure me that I am going to be okay?" In order to help them overcome these fears, we create a comprehensive financial plan that includes a "spending plan" to help them understand how the assets they are going to receive will help them live their new lifestyle along with achieve their goals.

I discovered that by providing clients with a fixed monthly budget instead of giving them quarterly or longer-term lump sum payments, some clients may have a more successful outcome. An example of this would be, after evaluating the client's total financial picture and developing her spending plan, we determined that her monthly budget would be $15,000. So, we decided that I would provide her with her funds ($45,000) quarterly and she managed the funds for the quarter. Unfortunately, this was a disaster because she had spent the entire quarter's budget within six weeks. Because she was used to being a financial delegator, she was having a difficult time managing the money on her own. We eliminated quarterly funds and began providing her with a monthly amount which for some financial delegating clients may be more successful.

What pitfalls or common mistakes should clients be aware of during this process?

Shannon Holland: One common mistake occurs during the division of retirement assets. For example, let's look at a husband who has had three jobs over the course of his lifetime and has never moved his 401K plans from any of those previous employers. We are now looking at three plans with a total of $250,000 in each plan. In addition, the wife has an IRA with $500,000 in it. In this scenario, most attorneys will immediately attempt to divide everything down the middle. In order to do this, a client ends up needing to do three separate QDRO'S (qualified domestic relations order) and dealing with three separate 401K providers to split the funds from each plan. This is where the knowledge of a financial planner is so beneficial. In this case, I would have the wife keep her IRA, the husband keep two of the three 401ks and then we just do one QDRO to split the remaining 401K. This eliminates the added stress, confusion, more money out of pocket, and a possible delay in obtaining the funds.

What inspired you to become a certified divorce financial planner?

Shannon Holland: There was a specific moment in my life that instilled a passion for wanting to help women that are often also financial delegators. When I was a child, my grandfather had passed away, leaving my grandmother with a few hundred acres of farmland and the farmhouse. Everything they owned was paid for, but they didn't have many liquid assets and had little cash flow from leasing out the farmland. Unfortunately, my grandmother fell ill and had to go into a Medicaid facility because she didn't have the liquid assets to pay for assisted living. I visited her one time at the assisted living facility and the conditions were terrible. To this day, I think about how different things could have been for her if she had someone help her develop a financial strategy that would have allowed her to live her remaining days with dignity. A loan could have been taken out on the farm or the farm could have been sold prior to her becoming ill to ensure proper funding to get her into a more dignified facility.

Proper planning helps to improve the quality of life for each of my clients. My main objective to this day is guiding people who are used to being financial delegators. Clients that are open to the help, responsive, and responsible and trusting enough to work closely with me to obtain financial success stories.

Can you share a lesson you learned early on that still impacts how you do business today?

Shannon Holland: A lesson that I learned very early on is to simply be a good listener. Ask meaningful questions so that you can easily identify the clients who are truly a good fit for your business and the services you can offer them. In this business, there are three types of clients. There are "do it yourself-ers," "collaborators," and as discussed throughout this chapter, financial delegators. "Do it yourself-ers" may or may not be a fit because they may or may not be open to help from outside sources. "Collaborators" may be open to some help, but they also seek advice from friends, family, etc., and, therefore, may or may not be a fit. The ideal client needs and is willing to receive my help. That's the financial delegator.

What is the most important question divorcing women should ask themselves as they consider financial planning?

Shannon Holland: Do I have all the right players on my team to successfully transition to this next stage of my life?

Let me start out by saying that all women are not financial delegators. In this day and age, a lot of the financial responsibility is shared. My wife, for example, is aware of all things financial in our lives and I make sure she has a complete understanding of what is going on. But some households are not like that, especially the baby boomer generation. For these women, it is crucial to have the right players lined up even before you file for divorce.

This brings to mind a woman who came to me as she was contemplating a divorce. After meeting with her a couple times, I referred her to a divorce attorney that I felt would be a good fit for her. She paid him a retainer, which she later got back due to working with me and developing a spending plan. Currently, she is becoming more confident and taking more control of the finances at home. Her husband sees this change in her, and the relationship is actually improving as a result.

Her dad was a successful businessman and gifts his daughters significantly each year. Instead of continuing to put this into the joint family account and use it for everyday living expenses, I advised her to open a separate account, which would be considered a non-marital account since the funds were provided directly from her dad and no marital assets were used in funding the account. In this way, money from her dad is being preserved for her and in the event the couple does decide to divorce, the money in that account is all hers. This is a prime example of having the right advisors in place even BEFORE divorcing. Financial advisors, psychologists, insurance agents, and tax experts are all important people who can help you transition smoothly to a new stage of life.

What is the most important thing divorcing women should consider when choosing/evaluating a potential financial planner?

Shannon Holland: In my opinion, it is important to find an advisor with the CFP™ credentials. Though CDFA®, Certified Divorce Financial Analyst credentialed planners have knowledge about divorce, the CFP certification provides more extensive training when it comes to the longer-term planning involved with divorcing couples.

How can someone find out more about Shannon Holland and how you can help?

Shannon Holland: The best way to reach me is via good, old fashioned phone call. My direct number is 239-513-6513. If you would prefer to reach me via email it is shannon@wiseriverweathmanagement.com. I look forward to empowering you on your quest for financial independence.

Opinions expressed in the attached article are those of the author and are not necessarily those of Raymond James. All opinions are as of this date and are subject to change without notice. Above case studies are for illustrative purposes only. Individual cases will vary. Any information is not a complete summary or statement of all available data necessary for making an investment decision and does not constitute a recommendation. Prior to making any investment decision, you should consult with your financial advisor about your individual situation.

Raymond James & Associates, Inc., Member New York Stock Exchange/SIPC

SHANNON HOLLAND, CFP(R), CDFA™, AIF(R)

Divorce Financial Planner

Associate Vice President, Investments

Wise River Wealth Management

Shannon Holland is a CERTIFIED FINANCIAL PLANNER™ practitioner, a Certified Divorce Financial Analyst™ and an Accredited Investment Fiduciary®

who specializes in financial planning and investment advisory services for women. He has many years of experience and an interdisciplinary knowledge of the financial issues that surround navigating life's changes. Shannon understands these changes and brings clarity to the complexities of these changes.

He credits his ability to help his clients separate the present from the past and set the standards for the future. The son of an Air Force non-commissioned officer, Shannon was born in Guam and raised in Maine, California and Virginia. He holds a BA degree from Virginia Tech, a Master's in Engineering from Old Dominion University and an MBA from the College of William and Mary. He served as a Lieutenant in the U.S. Army Reserves and draws on the strength of this military background to protect his clients' assets, alleviate fear of the future and proactively take steps to develop a plan to help them achieve their goals.

Shannon began his career in financial services at Wachovia Securities in 2002 and joined Raymond James in 2008. It is his goal to educate and encourage women to understand all financial options and to be involved in the financial decision-making process. Shannon not only guides his clients through the pros and cons of every financial decision during life's transitions, but also teaches them the basics of handling money and assets. He works closely with each client to provide sensitive, compassionate and personalized service, with the promise of maximum confidentiality.

With practical business knowledge and a track record of leadership and integrity, Shannon works closely with and guides clients to assure they take care of themselves financially while navigating life's changes. After the initial consultation, he works with clients to create a plan around what is most important to them and that aligns with helping them achieve their most important goals.

Shannon seeks to empower women to gainfully transition, achieve and maintain financial independence. He combines the analytical skills and attention to detail of an engineer with an experienced military officer's ability to develop and maintain trust, ensuring each client fully understands their financial situation and the jointly created plan for future financial success.

WEBSITE: www.wiseriverwealthmanagement.com

EMAIL: shannon@wiseriverweathmanagement.com

FAX: (239) 596-5474

PHONE: (239) 513-6513

ABOUT THE PUBLISHER

Mark Imperial is a Best-Selling Author, Syndicated Business Columnist, Syndicated Radio Host, and internationally recognized Stage, Screen, and Radio Host of numerous business shows spotlighting leading experts, entrepreneurs, and business celebrities.

His passion is discovering noteworthy business owners, professionals, experts, and leaders who do great work, and sharing their stories and secrets to their success with the world on his syndicated radio program titled "Remarkable Radio".

Mark is also the media marketing strategist and voice for some of the world's most famous brands. You can hear his voice over the airwaves weekly on Chicago radio and worldwide on iHeart Radio.

Mark is a Karate black belt, teaches kickboxing, loves Thai food, House Music, and his favorite TV shows are infomercials.

Learn more:
www.MarkImperial.com
www.ImperialAction.com
www.RemarkableRadioShow.com

www.ingramcontent.com/pod-product-compliance
Lightning Source LLC
Chambersburg PA
CBHW021239090426
42740CB00006B/602